Seven

INSIGHTS

to

ELEVATION

Thomas,
I love you and I
appreciate your
support always!
[signature]

JUANESE M. MOORE

First edition

Book design by Gen Y Digital
Author photography by Livelovetank

ISBN 978-1-7335063-0-4 (Paperback)
ISBN 978-1-7335063-1-1 (Ebook)

I want to dedicate this book to my son, Jared.
You have always been my reason for being,
for pushing myself to my next level.
You are my source and
I love you to infinity and beyond.
~Mom

To my family and friends whom I have
looked to for guidance and oftentimes vented to in this process,
Thank you, thank you, thank you!

Table of Contents

CHAPTER 1

Follow your inspired thoughts.

I specifically remember the day I started writing this book. I was in a car repair shop and I was moved to start writing my thoughts, feelings, and experiences. I had an overwhelming desire to write about what I have learned. I sincerely believe that when you have inspired moments, you should pursue them. You should go forward as you feel inspired because there is something great on the other side of the inspiration. Never in my life has this principle failed me. On the contrary, I have noticed that when inspired thoughts are not followed, opportunities are often missed. If you are inspired to read this book, please follow through on that inspiration. You will find something here specifically for you. Once you find it, you are fulfilling the intention of this book. This was written just for you to read at this specific time in your life. This inspired time.

When thinking about how to write the book, I knew that there were specific topics that needed to be discussed. This book is about how to take your life towards intentional growth . There are specific steps outlined here which allow for meaningful and fulfilling

1

progression of your life as you endeavor to push yourself toward your destiny. Please understand that this change is not a quick fix for anything. It is more like a new way of living. So it's not a diet, it's a healthy lifestyle. This book is like an outline, a guidebook, and a foundation that you can turn to if you find yourself lost or off track. The book is a culmination of experiences that I am sharing with you.

CHAPTER 2

Perception

Perception is a reflection of habits.

When you have any type of experience it will be viewed through the lens of your perception. It is an automatic response as each person's life and world is viewed through this lens. At times, your lens can be impacted by different situations and experiences which may or may not have been beneficial or productive for your life.

As we grow in our journey, we should be aware that we are viewing life through our own perception and others in the same situation will probably not see things the same way. We need to respect that. We don't necessarily need to agree with it or make it our own—just respect it. We need to remember we are dealing with another human being who has their own set of experiences and subsequent perceptions. Therefore, they are just as entitled to have their viewpoint as we are to have ours. Remember this as you grow. It will always be useful to you.

Perception is one of those words that people sometimes use without having a deeper level of understanding of its true meaning. This is not done intentionally of course, nonetheless, it happens all the time. Perception, in the sense I am referring to in this book, is simply how you view or understand things or situations. There is no right or wrong. Let me say this again. There is no right or wrong in perception. Right and wrong belong to judgment. Judgment is what keeps us from truly understanding others. We judge people based on our own beliefs which prevents us from productively engaging with people. Judgment is helpful in its own right, but we have to be careful how we exercise this as it can completely extinguish opportunities for new experiences and for productive relationships. Yes, you can say what is right or wrong for you. Absolutely. However, what is right for you may not be the same for those around you. Everyone gets to have their own perception and they don't all have to agree. It's similar to free will. We can do as we choose and with those choices come specific responsibilities and accountabilities.

Perception matters because it is how you view the world. On a more direct level, it is how you view everything that happens to and around you. It speaks to you on a very personal level as it reminds you of your past every time you have a new experience, thereby molding how you see, feel, and know things. It is what drives your responses and reactions. It helps to shape your values and beliefs. It actually molds you and grows you toward or away from what you believe to be good or bad for you. We make decisions all day based on what our insight tells us is right or good for us.

For example, did you ever meet or know someone who is always happy? It seems that no matter what, they are able to find something good in every situation. It almost seems like they are "golden," like they are The Chosen One. These people win contests, have great smiles, and others just seem to gravitate toward them. It would be easy to believe that nothing bad ever happens in their lives. Here's the thing about these people: they are viewing situations differently than the person who is always angry or always sad. They have made a conscious decision that their observations, reactions, and responses to situations must lead them to a more positive way of being. This subsequently impacts their opinion and they begin to see opportunities where obstacles lie. While this may feel annoying to those who don't share their views, it does not extinguish their zeal for life nor should it diminish their value as a human being. They are simply using their perception to enhance their experiences in life.

Countless studies have been done to show children raised in the same household will have different accounts of childhood experiences. Why? Because they may have actually had different experiences, but also their perceptions are different. You can take two children out to eat at a common burger joint. One may not like burgers, therefore the outing may seem skewed against them because they don't like burgers, despite the fact that they can also get chicken there. So if the family always eats burgers this child may grow up to think they were not loved or no one really took their feelings into consideration, which was likely not true. Nonetheless it is what the child believes. The other child may love burgers and feel that their parents showed them love by taking them to eat burgers, which also may or may not be true. This child will grow up to feel loved and accepted. The parents may have just been trying to accommodate everyone with this place. It was cost effective so this is why they chose it. The point may have been just for an outing or to not have to cook on Saturday, not as an exercise of attention or deflection to any of their children separately. However, perception can skew something this simple.

In understanding this, you can use your perception to help you create the life you actually want for yourself. Think about how you have used it in your life thus far. Do you often feel victimized or let down? Do you feel like everything is a struggle in your life? Do you live in the extremes (using *always* and *never* statements)? Or do you see through "rose-colored glasses" meaning that everything seems to be ok, regardless of circumstances? Do things always seem to work out for you? The answers to these questions will help you to identify how you view life. Please understand that I am well aware that good and bad happen to us all. What we do with what happens is shaped by perception. Let me give you an example.

I live in the metro Atlanta area and traffic is a big deal as I am sure it is in any metro area. When you have a person cut you off in traffic, are you immediately offended? Do you honk your horn and then then get into some "road rage" expressions of anger toward this unknown person? Most of us do. This is a perfect example of perception at work. If we stop to remember that whatever this person is doing has nothing to do with us our feelings may change. Perhaps this driver has a sick person laying in the back of their car and they are speeding to the ER. Maybe they just got a bad phone call and a loved one is sick or dead. Perhaps this person is having some type of medical issue themselves. At the end of the day, it has nothing to do with you. So why are you taking it so personally? How would you feel if you were dealing with any of these situations? Did your perception just change?

The reason I am sharing this is that I want you to really consider your life views. If you always feel like the world is against you, take another look. You are reading this book now, despite whatever may have happened to you in your life to prevent you from being here. And you have some type of resources which led you to this book. Take an honest look at where you are in your life and figure out how you got there, noting what worked well for you and what didn't. Then I want you to start to look for behaviors which can take you to your next level, whatever that is in your life. If you really do this work on your perception, you will go so much further than you thought. You will begin to view your life differently. You will see the things which did go your way and how they have helped/saved you. You will literally see your way out of victimization of yourself. Application of this technique allows you to begin to work in gratitude.

Deeper perception will lead you directly to gratitude. Being grateful allows for expansion. Think about it. How many times has this actually been demonstrated to you in some way? Refer to The Chosen One discussed earlier. This person literally seems to grow everything they touch or set their mind to. They get the promotions, bigger cars, bigger piece of pie, or whatever. They win. They win because their beliefs are different and they have learned to live in gratitude. See, their perception is a reflection of their habits. They are habitually productive and happy which means they set themselves up to succeed. When people want to succeed, they do more. They engage. They are happy because they learn how to turn frustrations into lessons. They look for the lessons in situations—then learn how to apply these lessons. Subsequently, they become grateful for the lesson which leads to living in gratitude. Negativity and gratitude exist only as opposing forces. If you are constantly negative in your interactions, you see nothing to be grateful for. You miss the lessons, missing the opportunities to learn and to grow.

Once you start to use this new perception, prepare yourself for what is to come as opportunities to exercise it will come right away. This is your black box warning. Things will start to happen which seem to be designed specifically to trip you up and get you back to your old way of thinking. It is similar to learning to ride a bike. Don't fret the fall as it is inevitable. Get up, dust yourself off, find the error, make the correction, visualize it going right, and execute. Changing is not an overnight process and takes work. It takes execution and consistency. Consistency will come if you know it is worth it for you—if you know having a positive outlook will get you closer to where you want to grow in your life. This is a life-changing habit you must develop and use for it to work. Habits take time to develop, right. With this one you will reap direct rewards. It will work if you work it.

Changing your perception may take you out of your comfort zone. It may feel uncomfortable to you at times. This is ok. Understand that there is no growth in your comfort zone anyway. This book is about growing to your next level, so discomfort will happen. It may be that you become isolated from family and/or friends. It may be that you are the only one working late at the office. It may often feel like you are the only one who sees your vision. It may get lonely. You will probably question yourself along the way and wonder why you are putting yourself through this as it feels like nothing is changing. Oh, but it is changing. Doubt is there to do its job which is to discourage and stop your progress. Don't let it. Understand its role in this process and keep pushing. The work itself may not be pretty, but nonetheless, you are working. You are still growing and getting stronger. This is working for you.

It is important that you remember something about this process. It is for you. Yes, there are people in your life who may directly benefit from your work, but this work must be about growing yourself. What I have found is that if you do this work for someone else, you may not be consistent. This work is for those who value themselves, regardless of what someone else may think. This value should not be attached to other's opinion of you or you will not stick to it. Others may not understand why you are doing this work or what you intend to gain from it. You define your own gain and intention. Not me or anyone else. Just be clear that you deserve it. Let your clarity be your guide.

CHAPTER 3

Victimization of Self

Pity parties are not powerful.

*N*ow that we understand how perception works, let's talk about how we set ourselves up to be victims. Yes, many of us do this to ourselves. How many times have you walked into a situation knowing that it would not be good for you, but you proceeded anyway? How many times have you said to yourself, "Something told me..." or "I had a feeling..."? Do you take your own advice? Do you take the advice of those who love you and have your best interest at heart? These are the questions we should consider when looking at the situations that we find ourselves in which make us feel victimized.

You are probably one of the nicest people you know. You go above and beyond for everyone and people love you. You are genuinely a good person. So why do you always find yourself in situations where people are taking advantage of your kindness and trying to use you? Are you tired of feeling this way? Well let's take a look at what is really going on so we can help you get out of the cycle of victimization which you seem to find yourself in.

When we think about victims, we often think of someone who

has suffered a terrible tragedy or a situation where someone fell prey to a scheme. This is true; however, let's work on our perception a little here. If you close your eyes right now and imagine what a victim looks like, they are probably lifeless or very hopeless looking— destitute if you will. Now close your eyes again and imagine what a survivor looks like. In my mind's eye, a survivor looks similar to Rambo—disheveled, dirty, and maybe even tired or injured—but alive with smoke billowing around them. Victims are typically connected with death as an end result. I have some great news for you. If the situation, scheme, or tragedy did not kill you then you are a survivor, not a victim.

Victimization of self means that somehow you have stripped yourself of total control, ending up with responsibility for nothing, including your responses. You created defenselessness and released your control and power. This lack of power, which you perceive to be your truth, means that you hold no responsibility for any part of what happened and any response you provide is justified because you have been victimized. Victimization of self removes accountability from you as your logic tells you that you are not even responsible for your reaction. The situation or problem was not created by you. And you did the best you could, given the circumstances. You were essentially and effectively stripped of all power, even over your thoughts and actions AND you were in agreement with this stripping of power. This happened because there is no room for powerful thought processes or actions when you are working in your own victimization.

For example, do you feel that people are always doing you wrong, despite the good will and intentions you have toward them? Do you feel that people always take from you? Do you think that no matter what you do things seem to never go your way? Does this make you feel sad and depressed at times because you feel like you are not in control of anything? If you are answering "yes" to these questions you are operating in the victimization of yourself. You often feel defeated and unappreciated. It actually feels like life is set up against you at times, and if it were not for bad luck you wouldn't have any luck at all. You are a good person and you do the things that good people do, but you still can't seem to catch a break. It seems that you have a target on your back for dysfunction and stress.

Take a moment and reread the previous paragraph. Where is the personal power in those statements? The answer is that there is none. Your power has been given away to others. Victimization of self includes handing over your power to situations and to other people. Let's see how a different perception can turn these situations around for you.

Your good intentions toward other people should be governed by you, not someone's response or reaction. Their response or reaction should teach you about who you are dealing with, but it should not govern your intentions. Why do you feel that people are always taking from you? Be specific when thinking about this and look for how you could have changed the outcome. If you couldn't, maybe people do like to take from you. If this is the case, I urge you to take a look at yourself, if this bothers you, and see where you can be more assertive. Are you comfortable with the word "no?" Do you use it at all? Are you open to trying it? In regards to things never going your way, what exactly is your way? Are you walking into situations with a planned outcome or do you believe that results are out of your control? How do you know what your way is if you don't plan for it or have the capability to define exactly what it is you are looking for? Typically a plan involves specific steps for accomplishing an end result. Do you know what those steps are and did you take them?

I have found that people will get "depressed" over situations, especially when engaging in victimization of self. Before you get upset, please understand that I am not denouncing depression as a real illness as I understand and know that it is. However, I also know that people will say that they are depressed when they simply did not get their way, or rather they did not put in the effort to create an expected outcome. This is called pouting, or perhaps manipulation, but not depression. Sometimes when people put in effort and things do not go their way, it leaves them feeling powerless. Commonly, people will slide into feeling powerless when frustrated as, unfortunately, it is an easier emotion to get to. See when we throw a pity party, as we all do at times, we are not being powerful. Pity parties are not powerful. They are quite the opposite as a matter of fact. They justify victimization and eliminate accountability. When you are trying to get to your next level in your life, there is no room for a pity party or prolonged feelings of powerlessness. These are the epitome of unproductive feelings and will get you nowhere fast, other than toward unproductive behaviors and away from your intentions. Your next level demands respect, accountability, and personal power.

So how do I work in respect, accountability, and personal power? The first step is that you must decide that you are worth it. In doing so, you need to also know that you have to give it to yourself first. It is illogical to expect someone to give you respect when you don't respect yourself. It is irrational to think that someone will believe that you hold power when you don't believe it yourself. You hold yourself accountable first and you will always do your personal best. In doing so, your personal best will only increase. I promise you it will. Understand, walking out of victimization of self takes courage. Some of those closest to you may not understand why you are behaving differently. They may even call you "crazy" for feeling that you deserve this. That's okay too. Remember perception. They are working from their own, not yours. We will talk more about naysayers later; however, it is important to remember not to give them your power. Keep it for yourself as you will need it.

When you make the decision to no longer be a victim, you are innately giving yourself power. You will instinctively start to look for your power over and in situations. Keep in mind, this is not done in an unproductive or selfish manner. You are not seeking power to control other people. Instead, you are looking to gain control over yourself, your responses, and your life. Keep the focus on your part and know that when you are coming out of self-victimization, it is a very self-reflective activity. You have to look at yourself and work to find your part. Find your lesson in the situation and then move on. This is so important, as owning your part will give you back responsibility and accountability. Taking back responsibility and accountability mean that you are taking your personal power back from whoever or whatever you gave it to. When you take your power back, you are no longer a victim. You are on your way!

CHAPTER 4

Negative Nelly

There is no growth in the destruction of others.

Now that you are working on enhancing your perception and coming out of your self-victimization, let's talk about some of the resistance you may get. This resistance may come in the form of a person who you believed would support you in your journey or someone who has been in your life for a long time. Lately it seems that since you have decided to undertake this transitional journey this person always has a snide remark or something negative to say. They may want you to continue to do the same things you have always done with them, like eat out a lot or going out every weekend. They will have solid reasons why you should not change and you may feel that you owe this person an explanation for your decision and subsequent actions toward the decision you have made. They may tell you that you are "acting new" and will have you second-guessing your decision. You may feel like you will lose their love, friendship, or companionship if you continue to make the changes that you have been making. If you have identified this person or persons, you have just identified your Negative Nelly.

Please understand this: I am not saying that this person does not love you. In fact, they may love you so much that they are afraid for you as you journey into this new life of yours. They may be afraid they will lose you or afraid to make the same changes for themselves. They may live and operate in fear, which leaves them with pervasive negativity. They, most often, do not mean to be this way and they usually don't mean you harm as they do love you. Eventually, this person or group of people will accept the new you and will probably secretly envy you for having the nerve to make the changes you are making. They have no problem reminding you that they love you and only want the best for you. But, try as they might, they just do not have your vision or your perception. So they work to try to protect you from yourself.

In the past, your Negative Nelly was probably your biggest fan. At some point they may have held the role of pushing you and helping you in any way they could. Again, most of the time they love you in their own way. Oftentimes they see in you what they wish they had or wish they could be. They have usually had your back at some point in your life which is why you spend time with them, and why they have some sort of influence over you now. You probably hold them very dear to your heart. And this hold—the love you have for this person—is why it matters how they feel about you. While we all like to say that we don't care what people think of us, the reality is that we do care how certain people feel about us and we value their opinions. If your Negative Nelly is one of those people for you, it will be difficult to push past their opinion and do what you feel is right for yourself as you grow. You are a good person and you don't want to hurt anyone. Somehow it may feel that if you push forward, you will lose this person in your life. You don't have to lose them at all. You may have to adjust the type of influence they have on you and whether or not they should have any at all based on what you are trying to accomplish. At this point, you should use your better judgment regarding this relationship and don't stop your growth process.

When we seek approval from the people who mean a lot to us, it is like we are seeking validation from them. We want them to tell us that we are making the right decision for our own lives. While it is good to get advice from others at times, it is important that we consider the source, especially if we are undertaking something that is new to them as well. Again, oftentimes the Negative Nelly will be working in their own fear which they are projecting onto you. This will reflect itself in the advice they give to you. Usually, they don't mean you any harm. Still, I urge you to not allow their fear to negatively impact your decision to grow. Wouldn't it be great if you could show them that their fears are unfounded and that they can experience their own growth too? Perhaps this would strengthen them in a productive manner and you all can grow together. However, if this is not the case, you keep going and make a conscious decision regarding the role this person will play in your future decision-making processes. Understand, you don't have to throw the baby out with the bathwater—you can keep the relationship. You just have to decide how much of your energy to give it.

Thus far I have been discussing Negative Nellies who don't actually mean to be negative. Keep in mind though, that there are people out there who are just jealous and self-centered. Their main agenda is to get to where they feel they need to be at any cost, which includes harming you if it seems that you are blocking them in some way—real or imagined. At this point, if you are using your perception regularly, you should have a feeling about who these people may be in your life. Do what you need to do, but please do it in a good spirit. Don't work to demean or belittle people. Make sure you do your part to leave them feeling whole. There is no real and sustainable growth in the destruction of others, so please be mindful of your intentions and keep them pure.

The last thing I want to say about Negative Nelly is that he or she has a role in your growth. How? You may ask. Well, if we are dealing with a Negative Nelly who is truly trying to look out for you, you have to learn how to manage interpersonal relationships in your growth, understanding that everyone is not taking the journey with you and it may not be due to ill will. Your approach with this person(s) can be pivotal for you as it can teach you how to use discernment effectively. You have to be able to separate the Nelly who loves you and is working in their own fear from the Nelly who simply isn't. These people probably play different roles in your life now and you have to make an informed decision about how they are going to be involved in your future, if at all. No one can make this decision for you. This is where you are making choices based on your gut instincts and you have to trust yourself.

Trusting yourself involves using a measure of self-control to make decisions. You want to make decisions exercising good will, doing what you intend to be the best outcome for all involved. When you operate in this manner, you are open to criticism just as you are with any other decision you have made in your life. The difference now is that you are using your instinct and your perception in a more productive way—you are learning to trust yourself and the decisions that you are making. Using self-control means that you are able to hear the criticism and opinions of others without "getting in your feelings" about what is being said as you understand now that people are able to communicate based on their own perception. Stay true to your intention and work with good will and your self-control will grow, further strengthening your personal power and your ability to work in it.

CHAPTER 5

Truth

The truth is the purest form of communication.

T ruth is a very interesting concept. Oftentimes, people make the truth subject to what they need it to be. Amazingly, you may find that this truth changes depending on the day and the person you are talking to. Perception, as we discussed before, can definitely have an impact on one's truth. A simple fact that I love about the truth is that it needs no friends or allies. Additionally, the truth does not require the belief of anyone. At any time. It stands alone.

People often wonder if the truth can be subjective. It is actually more about perception. See, my "truth" will be different from your "truth" in certain situations as our experiences influence our perceptions, which can then influence how we see things, our respective truths. For example, if you see a person crying you may think that they are emotionally hurt and sad when really the person is overjoyed about something—the tears are happy tears. This is your perception at work. The truth is simply that the person is shedding tears, but our experiences and beliefs lead us to make presumptions about the situation. Perhaps your experience with people crying was centered around pain and sadness. This is your truth; however, it is not always the truth and certainly not the truth for the person crying tears of joy.

As we look at situations to try to find our truth, it is automatically going to be swayed and influenced by our experiences. So when seeking the truth, work to remove your experiences from (and expectations of) the situation so that you can get to the core of what you are dealing with. If I could allude to the traffic example earlier, at the end we discovered that our truth is fueled by our perception in situations as simple as dealing with traffic. We found that the truth can be completely misconstrued. Perception can lead us to circumstantial thinking. We have to remember this when looking for the truth so that we are not influenced by what we think is happening. Instead, the truth requires us to look at what actually is happening without any influences. The truth is the truth all by itself. Yes, it can be difficult to accept and it can push your belief system, but it's still just the truth. So simple. I am not trying to sell you anything; however, there is something you should always remember. You are worth the truth every day and in every situation.

People you engage with deserve the truth as well. Get in the habit of always giving the truth as this frees you from trying to remember the lie. The truth is the purest form of communication. Everything else is literally just sprinkles (cute, but no real value and can be a constant distraction). Stop letting people sprinkle all over you, literally. Go deeper. Think deeper. Love deeper. Be deeper. That's where the truth lives, your truth. The more you do this, the easier it becomes. Trust me, I learned this one the hard way.

Living in truth can be a challenge within itself as obstacles will show their faces again to try to shake your truth. Remember, obstacles are tools. Become convicted in your truth. As you do this, learn in truth and keep loving in truth. What I mean is do not become cocky or arrogant. Do not become so rigid that you cannot deal with people who don't live in their truth or won't accept yours. As you grow in truth and perception, you will develop empathy. Be empathetic and don't judge. At the same time, don't fear the loneliness which will certainly accompany the truth. Loneliness can cause you to compromise your truth. Don't let the loneliness be a distraction or detract you from this journey. When you rest on the truth, you will engage in a pure form with people. If the truth bothers them, it literally has nothing to do with you. This part is crucial as people may try to convince you that you are "different" or "acting like you don't care." These sentiments typically come from people who have not learned to live in the truth. Again, it has nothing to do with you. Don't be manipulated into believing that it does. It is typically fruitless to try to convince people of anything which is outside of their belief system. I think I already mentioned that I am about productive behaviors, as you should be while you work on your greatness.

Dealing with and living in the truth can appear to be a cold and uncaring way to live. Contrarily, living in the truth allows you the opportunity to see things simply as they are. Subsequently, you get to guide and manage your own behaviors accordingly. This requires the use of self-reflection to consider the productivity of our own actions and change them if they are found to be working in the opposite direction of what we want. For example, if we want to take some weight off, there are some specific behaviors or habits that should be addressed to assist us, if it is a meaningful goal. These habits or behaviors may seem difficult to develop. Please remember that the level of difficulty does not negate the necessity. As you embrace this concept you begin to live in your own truth.

You will get to a point in your life where you want your truth to work for you. It will be like it is calling you toward what you need to focus on. You will feel frustrated often and won't know why. You will get tired of feeling tired. At that point, it's time to really work. It's time to stop with the excuses and just do the work which will propel you to your greater self. This requires you to focus on your truth, which means that you need to identify what it is. You need to get comfortable with it and settle into it. The only way your truth can work for you in a productive manner is if you stop fighting it. Your truth is the little voice—the nudging that may not make sense at the time. Later you realize you should have listened to it. I say little voice because the truth doesn't have to be loud or boisterous to make its point. It is sometimes like a whisper of destiny. Go with it—no excuses.

When looking at the truth and how it works, people often expect for it to be a logical situation. This can be far from reality. The truth is not encumbered with your expectation of what it should be. It just is. Understanding this fact helps us as we learn to work in the truth.

The interesting thing about the truth is that it won't change whether you listen to it or not. It is still the truth, now and forever. As much as we try to make it a subjective reality, it still remains the truth despite your acceptance, ignorance, or denial of it. Logic does not always apply and that is the truth. See, it doesn't make logical sense that I am even writing this book if you look at my past choices, decisions, and behaviors. It doesn't make sense that you are reading this book either based on your past. But nonetheless we are both here, which is pure truth in this moment. We are here because we are working in our truth. Interesting—sounds like destiny.

The truth is that it is not easy to live in truth. It is not easy to follow nudges from destiny as they don't always make sense. You don't see how it can happen. People say, wonder, and think that you are behaving outside of what they believe you should be doing—despite what the truth is telling you, despite what your gut is telling you, despite what you know to be your truth in that moment. What happens is we feel the need to validate other people's feelings, then we begin to minimize ourselves so that others can accept us. And that is the truth. See, the truth will take you against the grain and it will make you question everything you have learned, everything you know. But if you do—if you take this chance on yourself and walk into your truth—then prepare yourself for elevation.

The truth does not change in and of itself. Instead, it elevates you. Truth pushes you to your next level of life because it will not minimize itself to suit whoever your Negative Nelly is at any given moment in time. It remains steadfast and true every day. When you are ready to live in the truth, you will know. Open yourself to your new reality and run baby. Run toward it and get your life. It's been waiting for you. You have been playing with yourself, sprinkling on yourself. It's time to stop minimizing yourself and, to instead, grow higher.

Now, people will try to discourage you and will want you to explain yourself and your new thought process. Don't feel obligated to do so. Remember, your life, your truth. You don't owe anyone anything. I know you won't intentionally hurt anyone because the truth does not work to inflict pain. It actually brings clarity. This clarity may be painful, but then we are dealing with another concept called acceptance. You are not responsible for how or even if people accept you. You are only responsible for your intention. Keep your intention pure and you will be fine. When dealing with your truth, remember that it does not exist to hurt or to infringe upon another person's truth. Stay with the intention of truth—clarity. This will help you to live an unapologetic life in your truth—every day and in every situation.

CHAPTER 6

Confidence

Be humble and have self-appreciation at the same time.

id you ever meet someone who just seemed to have everything in their life together? From all practical perspectives, it seemed that this person was someone to emulate because they seemed to not have a care in the world. They walked into the room and people stopped and gave them attention in some form. They had a great personality and seemed so calm and in control. To you they were a walking definition of confidence and you thought, "I wanna be like them when I grow up." Well sweetheart, time to grow up!

Confidence, as referred to in this book, is self-assurance from appreciating your own qualities. Let's break this concept down so we can see what we are really dealing with here. Self-assurance means being assured from within yourself. Assured is comforted, encouraged, and protected. Appreciating your own qualities means that you can identify yourself (who you are, what you can do, what you stand for) and then subsequently appreciate what you have identified. Let's think about appreciation for a moment. How do you show appreciation to others? Do you respect people you appreciate?

Do you listen and respond to people who you appreciate? Do you honor their name when you speak of them? Do you change how you talk, speak, or act when around the people you appreciate? Identify how you treat people who you appreciate and then I want you to turn these behaviors inward. This is not done as an act of selfishness or as a way to be boastful. Instead, it is an act of self-awareness and self-love.

Now let's clarify this definition of confidence as we have identified it above. Confidence is being comforted, encouraged, and protected from within yourself while appreciating who you are, what you can do, and what you stand for. This is a lot deeper than we thought when we checked out that person walking in the room. There is work involved in confidence. You should bestow upon yourself the adoration and respect you put into admiring others. Reflect on this and see where you need to work.

Confidence is not easily earned or kept. It's not something that once you have you get to keep it forever. You have to work on it. You have to check it regularly. You have to keep working. Confident people are people who have worked to earn and keep their confidence. They did not just wake up like that and start walking into rooms dazzling people. They may have even practiced their walk so that they didn't trip over their feet in their entrance. You wouldn't know that they had to work on their walk if they did not tell you, yet they understood the value of the work. Confident people are hard workers. They have earned their confidence. Now don't confuse them with arrogant people. Arrogant people are typically the exact opposite in that they don't have a lot of confidence at all. The arrogance is simply their front, their coping mechanism. Don't take their arrogance personally as it has nothing to do with you. As far as confidence is concerned, please know and understand that it comes with work and it leaves without work. If you stay consistent with yourself in regards to this work, you will reap the benefits.

How do you get confidence? Well, you have you start within yourself. It is not an externally driven trait. If you work on developing your confidence with the expectation that people will congratulate you, then you can stop now because it doesn't work that way. You have to learn how to be humble and have self-appreciation at the same time. You have to be willing to do the work without getting noticed or appreciated from others. You have to be willing to stay focused when distractions will surround you, intentional or not. You have to be willing to be self-reflective so that you can find areas in your life that you need to put work into. And you have to be able to do all this without fail, all the time, and in all situations.

You must hold yourself to a higher standard because that is where you are trying to go. The higher standard is not for everyone, that's why it's higher. Some people are not even aware that it is there. Others see it but convince themselves that it is not attainable so they don't work at all. They talk themselves out of their own truth. Then you have those that will do the work. To get confidence and to sustain it, you have to be willing to not only see and acknowledge the higher level, you gotta be willing to work for it. You have to. There is no easy way. This book is to help guide you, but the real work is in the application of the principles discussed here. Reading this book is just the first step.

Confidence comes when you start working in your truth. We talked about truth and we know that it elevates. Elevation means that you are going higher. Working in confidence means that you are working to take yourself to a higher level. Elevation is what we are working on here. As such, we need to do all the work we discussed in the previous chapters. Work on your perception and if you find yourself in a constant state of victimization, take yourself out. Handle your Negative Nellies. Then walk into and work on your truth. Confidence will come. Guaranteed. Look back at the definition. You are assured, appreciative, and respectful of yourself. If you are not feeling this way about yourself, then truthfully, you are not confident. So why not?

I work as a therapist and I regularly talk to people about how others treat them and how it impacts their self-esteem. Most people will say that they have good self-esteem and that they don't need any work in that area. If your self-esteem is attached to others' acceptance of you, your ideals, your desires, and your wants, then you are not working in self-esteem. You are gauging your esteem of yourself based on others. This is actually not self-esteem. So if self-esteem is not yours, you cannot have true confidence. This is where you can stop and do more self-evaluation. Go back to perception and evaluate your work. Are you still easily offended? Are you judgmental of others? Are you easily swayed by what is popular right now and feel that you need to engage in whatever is the "in" thing right now?

If you answered "yes" to any of these questions there is more work to do to get to confidence. I can assure you if you do the work you will get there.

Once you get there, you will feel more calm and in control. Your decisions will be made with tranquility and you will flow better in your daily life. Think about it. Confident people tend to bring order to a chaotic situation. Oftentimes they are identified as the calm in the storm. Why do they seem so composed? In reflecting on the definition of confidence, please recall that we found that these people feel protected and comforted. These feelings evoke calming behaviors. Do confident people get nervous? Absolutely. The difference is that they know their worth is based on their own assessment and not the opinion of people they don't know. They have done the work and they know they have. They are comforted in this knowledge. They are secure in their ability to handle what is coming their way. They also have no problem telling you if they are nervous as they are not worried about whether or not you are judging them.

We have discovered that confident people are hard workers and we now understand that confidence requires consistent work. You have to guard your work, protect it, and reinforce it. Once you strengthen your self-esteem and confidence, expect that Negative Nelly is on her way and she feels that she has work to do. Know that others who have not done the work will judge you. You may even have people from your past come forward to remind you of who you were before. Please know that this is par for the course and should be expected. Don't let this rattle you and take your focus. You are now working in and on your truth. Don't stop when someone tries to test you. Go ahead and rest assured that you can handle this. You have prepared yourself for the test.

CHAPTER 7

Permission

It is counter-productive to seek to grow without guidance and support

When we think about putting all the principles into play that we are discussing in this book, we need to consider permission. This is because of how some of us are conditioned to function in life. We tend to work within the parameters of permission. As children, we needed permission to do pretty much anything that we wanted to do. The need for permission carried over into adulthood via jobs and responsibilities. So as we venture into a new way of thinking and being, who is going to give us permission? Is there approval that we need from someone in order for us to make these changes? Is there someone in your life who will be disappointed about the changes you are making? If so, will their opinion impact your decision to continue?

For the sake of clarity, permission is simply allowance to do or be. As an adult, we pretty much move around in our lives within the parameters of what is expected of us and of what is deemed to be "normal." These parameters or set of societal/cultural norms shape how we live our lives. Some of the topics discussed in this book may be different from what is your established norm. If so, you have to determine how to move forward. Are you going to proceed because you see value in the changes you want to make or are you going to stay within the guidelines already established for you because they are working better for you? In the discussion of permission, it is important that you answer this question as you will need to address it at some point within yourself.

The source of your permission is solely dependent upon you. For some, there is no one. If you are in this group of people, you tend to move to the beat of your own drum. You tend to not seek approval or even acceptance from anyone. Therefore, it really does not matter to you if anyone likes what you are doing as you make your own decisions. You can comfortably defend your decisions if necessary. For others, permission may come from family members or friends. This group of people tends to move together and work with collective thinking as a guide. You won't do it if your friends or family don't approve or understand why you feel you need something more than what is provided by the group. On a larger scale, permission can come from cultural expectations or norms. For example, if your culture dictates that your actions must be approved of by a parent or governing body, then that is who you seek permission from whether you ask directly or through indirect compliance with previously established standards. As you read this chapter and contemplate making whatever changes you deem necessary for your elevation, you will need to identify who you will seek permission from, if anyone.

Some of you may ask why you even need to get permission. This, again, is an individual decision. Some may feel compelled to obtain approval. If so, do what you need to do so that you can walk into the changes you need to make with a clear and focused mind. Otherwise, you will not be centered and you may not be devoted to making the changes you identified which would take you higher. If you don't feel compelled to seek permission, then don't.

It's important for me to share that permission does not necessarily mean specifically asking someone if you can do this. It can be in the form of getting a second opinion about what you want or need to do for yourself. We all need and should seek guidance as opening up yourself for guidance is a part of maturity and growth. This book is about growth and it would be counter-productive to seek to grow without guidance and support. No one should undertake this journey completely alone as it can be challenging and you will need, if nothing else, someone to vent to.

CHAPTER 8

Strength and Courage

Challenge yourself to be the person you are trying to be.

s transformation in the way you live and think is undertaken, you must be committed to the work, understanding that it is a process. Most processes include a certain amount of failure. Failure will provide the best lessons, if we are open to them. Unfortunately, failure can also cause you to feel discouraged. Because you have come this far, you will look for the lessons and you will do the necessary self-evaluation to grow. Fear of failure can open your mind to self-doubt and feeling discouraged along the way. When these negative feelings happen, as they inevitably will, you must have the strength and courage to continue—to stay the course. You have to understand that this journey is not for everyone and it is certainly not for the faint of heart or insecure.

Strength is interesting in that you can derive strength from different external sources like family and friends. Courage, as well— we feel encouraged when others notice our work and acknowledge it in some way. While this support feels good and can keep you going for a while, at some point it will get quiet. At some point people will tire and they may fade away momentarily. What happens then? What happens when the cheering section gets quiet? Can you continue your work? Will you continue your work? Having a personal reason will help you during these times. Why are you doing this? Why do you want this? Why you? Why now? Why do you think it will make you better? Answer these questions for yourself and you will surely find your strength and courage.

In answering the noted questions, it is important to consider who is pushing you to do this. I implore you to consider yourself as the source. What if, for whatever reason, the person you noted were not with you? Would you continue or would you give up? The work is yours and yours alone. We acknowledged before that others will be impacted by your work. Understanding this, what happens if the person who you assigned the task of providing you with strength and courage disagrees with what you are trying to do in your life? What if they like your status quo and don't want you to make any changes, even though you know the changes you are making evolve you as a person? How would you handle this? I pose these questions to you because they are very real possibilities and can impact your growth in a positive or negative way.

As you truthfully answer all the questions posed above, understand that it will take some courage and strength to be honest with yourself. It is okay if you don't like the answers you have right now because you can change them. That's the cool part about self-reflection and self-awareness. First you find out what you actually know and acknowledge that it has impacted your behavior. Then you can change your behavior if you want a different outcome. This is a core component of this work. You are actually using your strength and courage in this moment. As such, it takes a strong person to complete self-reflective activities because it means that you are exposing your vulnerabilities. It means that you have to admit that you are not perfect, that you are somehow a flawed person. It takes courage to admit this. Forget any stigma you previously carried as we all have a past. As long as you are breathing you have an opportunity to grow and change into who you want to be. I have found that judgment is often the source of why people don't grow or change. The fear of what others may think can be crippling. So often we do this to ourselves. Instead of setting ourselves up to succeed, we self-sabotage. This ends now.

As you ponder the answers noted you may not like the responses you give. This is okay as it presents the perfect opportunity to work. It presents an opportunity for you to grow into who you are going to be. If you do not see room for improvement, then you are either perfect or not being truthful with yourself. As a human being I know that a proclamation of perfection from me about me would mean that I am not being truthful with myself. It would mean that I am in denial. My preference is to live in awareness so that I am more productive and intentional in what I say and what I do. This allows me to support my personal growth. This is exactly what I desire for you as well.

Have you ever pushed yourself to complete something which seemed very intimidating? How did you feel afterward—did you feel courageous? Strong? Most often, we are stronger than we think. We just need to be challenged to see what we can do. Some of us actually thrive in a challenge and outperform our own expectations. When this happens, courage and strength are working together. Courage tells us to just try despite all the reasons it seems impossible. It urges us on and says, "Try anyway—you don't have anything to lose." Strength then steps up and says, "You got this." They are like a tag team that work together to help you overcome whatever you are seeing as an obstacle or challenge. I implore you to let them do their job. Let them work and reap the benefits of the work that they put in for you. Courage and strength are like your own personal soldiers to push you through when you just don't feel like it anymore. Let them work for you.

Now that you have figured out how to use them together, you have to keep them working together. It is akin to maintaining your vehicle. You can gas it up and drive it for a while, but at some point maintenance has to be done to keep it in tip-top shape. Challenge yourself regularly to be the person you are trying to be, especially when it feels uncomfortable. Walk in your truth. You did so much work to get there, don't let it be for naught.

Using all of these traits and skills on a regular basis will become a habit once you start. Just as you enjoy the feeling of overcoming your challenges, you will enjoy knowing that you actually have the strength and courage to do what you need to do to take yourself to whatever your higher level is. Once you get there I challenge you—no I dare you—to go even higher.

CHAPTER 9

Conclusion

Your next level: experience yourself in a way that you only dreamed was possible.

As I close this book, I am urged to go back to the beginning. I want to make sure that the intention of this voyage is maintained and understood. I want to make sure that this book is an effective read for everyone who picks it up. I want to make sure that the concepts are easy to understand and apply. I want you to feel empowered to make the changes that you need to make in your own life to take yourself to your next level. That's the intention—your elevation.

What is your next level? What does it look like to you? What do you need to get there? And finally, what is stopping you? Are you afraid of the work? Are you mentally strong enough? How do you know that you are strong enough? Do you have lessons that you can use and apply? What has kept you from applying them thus far? Did you deal with this situation or is it capable of further stalling you? Are there people who you need to pull back from because you know they are not going to understand and they are simply not ready for the new you? If so, what will keep you from refocusing your energy on those who will be your biggest cheerleaders? Are you really ready to commit to yourself, to your own growth, despite what others may say or believe? Do you believe in your vision? Do you believe in your next level? Do you believe you deserve it? Are you really ready for it?

These questions may sound very pointed and almost invasive. Let me explain the intention. These are questions that you must ask yourself and you must be honest in the responses. The answers will help to prepare you. They are like the foundational work that must be done so you don't sabotage your own efforts. I believe in setting yourself up to succeed, not to fail. When you set yourself up to succeed, you need to be able to answer the hard questions as they hold the keys to your success. Setting yourself up to succeed means that you have to be honest with yourself because you deserve it. You undoubtedly need honesty so you know what work you need to do and where you need to focus your precious energy.

Focus is necessary when you are trying to change your life, especially for the better. There are so many people who have shared and demonstrated how focus is key to success. I could do a whole chapter on who said what about focus and how it worked for them in their lives. This is a monumental concept and one that all of us have to deal with at some point in our lives. The key is to recognize when you are not focused and to make the correction. Find the thing in your in your life that blocks your productivity. When I completed this exercise my distraction was phone games. I use puzzle games to unwind; however, unwinding is one thing, but distracting me from productive work is something completely different. You have to know the difference, which means you have to be honest with yourself. Tell the truth, then make the correction. So I took back my power and deleted the games. If it takes too much energy or time from what should be happening, you have to let it go. Don't look back in time and find that games and other foolishness predominated your day, your life. That, my dear, would be 100 percent your fault and very tragic. Don't let your gifts sit unused and unexplored. This waste leads directly to feeling unfulfilled and could lead to a depressive state of mind if you are not careful.

Understand that applying the principles noted in this book in your life does not preclude you from bad situations. There are many different reasons we go through things in our lives, but I am a firm believer that none are intended to break you, only to make you stronger. Sometimes things happen as distractions simply to test the commitment that you have made to yourself. Big dreams require big work. There is no get-rich-quick plan or easy road. I tell people if you are getting no resistance, you are following the crowd. Resistance is designed to make you stronger. Are you committed to your next level or are you the same old you with big dreams and little work? This may sound harsh and somewhat judgmental, but please understand that this sword has a double edge. Talking the talk is easy, anybody can do it. I am talking about walking the walk, and this stroll is not for everyone. Nor is it for those who are easily offended. Knowing what you need to do to set yourself up to succeed is essential to being successful. I am only interested in your success, understanding and knowing that it is not as easy as it sounds, but it is so worth it.

Have you ever wanted something so badly that you could actually taste it? What did it feel like when you finally got it? Were you happy? Excited? Did you feel accomplished? Did you believe in yourself and what you could actually accomplish if you set your mind to it? What I want you to understand is that pushing towards your next level will leave you feeling like you love yourself on a deeper level. This growth, this change that you are making in your life is so worth it. You will find that you are growing into the new you and will experience yourself in a way that you only dreamed was possible. You will walk better, smile better, look better, and feel better. You will think better and your actions will be more deliberate and guided by what you need to do to continue these wonderful feelings that you have opened up within yourself. I am not telling you something that I have not experienced for myself. It is like opening what you know to be a gift that you have wanted for a very long time. Essentially it is what you are doing. You are opening you. You've been holding yourself back, setting yourself up to fail, living up to other people's expectations, and not really fulfilling your own needs. You've been who everybody else needs you to be and now it's time for you to be who you actually are. This may or may not coincide with what others want from you, expect from you, or need from you. However, it is who you are. Embrace it. Love it. Roll around in it. And just be.

In the midst of writing this book, I have had some life-changing experiences happen in my life and in the life of my son. You know, life can come for you and shake everything up in a way that you never expected and serve you one of your biggest fears on a platter.

He is okay now and will get better. I am urging him, constantly, to learn from this situation and to not only learn from it, but to apply the lessons. See, what I have found is that it really does not matter what you learn as you go through life if you are not willing to immediately and effectively apply the lessons that you learn. The change happens in the awareness as well as the application of the knowledge that you gain about yourself.

What I have found in my life is that the application of life's lessons is the hard part. I have also learned that using our experiences and lessons is crucial to our survival. The knowledge that we gain throughout our lives, throughout our experiences, is there to help us to grow. Things do not happen haphazardly or without reason. Your experiences in life were designed specifically for you in order to grow you toward what is meant for you. You have the knowledge within yourself regarding what you need to do more or less of, and to change to get to where you are supposed to be. This book serves as a guide. The principles are foundational so you can set yourself up to succeed. When used and actually applied, they work.

At this point, you have received foundational work. Understanding and applying these principles can set you up to succeed at your pursuits. It is now up to you to begin using them. It may be easy for some and for others it may be more challenging. What I want you to understand is that it is important to try. Your next level is attainable. You may have to revisit different sections at different times. This is the nature of life. Don't beat yourself up. Find the lesson and continue to your success!

Made in the USA
Columbia, SC
24 February 2019